533
TOC

CPS—MORRILL SCHOOL

Experiments with air.

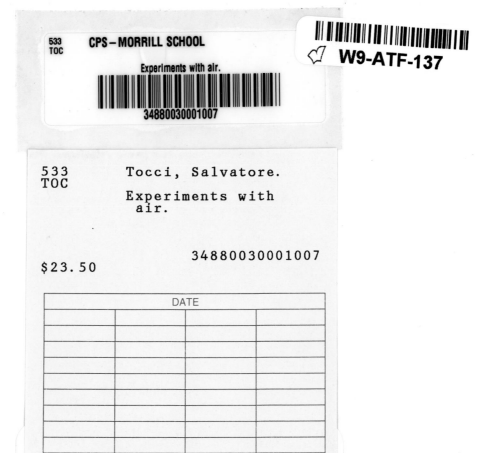

34880030001007

533
TOC

Tocci, Salvatore.

Experiments with air.

34880030001007

$23.50

DATE			

CPS—MORRILL SCHOOL
CHICAGO PUBLIC SCHOOLS
6011 S ROCKWELL STREET
CHICAGO, IL 60629
02/19/2004

BAKER & TAYLOR

EXPERIMENTS WITH AIR

A TRUE BOOK®

by

Salvatore Tocci

Children's Press®

A Division of Scholastic Inc.

New York Toronto London Auckland Sydney
Mexico City New Delhi Hong Kong
Danbury, Connecticut

Wind fills the sails of these sail boats as they race across a bay.

Reading Consultant
Nanci R. Vargus, Ed.D
Primary Multiage Teacher
Decatur Township Schools
Indianapolis, Indiana

Science Consultant
Robert Gardner

The photo on the cover shows hot air balloons. The photo on the title page shows flags blowing in the wind in front of the United Nations Building in New York City.

The author and publisher are not responsible for injuries or accidents that occur during or from any experiments. Experiments should be conducted in the presence of or with the help of an adult. Any instructions of the experiments that require the use of sharp, hot, or other unsafe items should be conducted by or with the help of an adult.

Library of Congress Cataloging-in-Publication Data

Tocci, Salvatore.
    Experiments with air / Salvatore Tocci.
      p. cm. – (A True Book)
    Includes biographical references and index.
    Summary: Explores the properties of air and air pressure through ten simple experiments using everyday objects.
      ISBN 0-516-22511-1 (lib. bdg.)   0-516-29362–1 (pbk.)
      1. Air—Experiments—Juvenile literature. [1. Air—Experiments.
2. Experiments.]   I. Title. II. Series.
QC161 .T63 2002
533'.6'078—dc21
                                                            2001004915

© 2002 by Children's Press
A Division of Scholastic Inc.
All rights reserved. Published simultaneously in Canada.
Printed in the United States of America.

CHILDREN'S PRESS, AND A TRUE BOOK®, and associated logos are trademarks and or registered trademarks of Grolier Publishing Co., Inc. SCHOLASTIC and associated logos are trademarks and or registered trademarks of Scholastic Inc.

1 2 3 4 5 6 7 8 9 10 R 11 10 09 08 07 06 05 04 03 02

Contents

This girl knows the apple is real because she can see, smell, taste, touch, and hear the apple as she eats it.

How Do You Know It's Real?

Have you ever heard the expression "seeing is believing"? Perhaps a friend has told you something that you found impossible to believe. You may have said that you wouldn't believe it unless you saw it for yourself. People sometimes don't accept that something is real unless they can see it with their own eyes.

Your eyes are only one way that you can sense what is real. You actually depend on five **senses**—seeing, smelling, hearing, tasting, and touching—to determine that something is real. For example, smells coming into your bedroom from the kitchen may tell you that dinner is being prepared. Sounds coming from outside may tell you that your friends are riding their bikes. You believe these things are real

These children can't sense the air surrounding them. How can they know it's really there?

because you can smell the food and hear your friends.

Can something be real if you cannot see, smell, hear, taste, or touch it? There is something that is very real, but usually none of your senses can detect it, even though it is all around you. It is air.

How Can You Tell Air Is There?

There are days when you can feel the wind. Even though you can't see it, you can feel the air blowing against your face. Is there some way of knowing that the air is there when it isn't blowing?

You know the air is real when it blows against your face.

Taking Up Space

You will need:
- funnel
- glass jar
- modeling clay
- measuring cup
- pencil

Place the spout of the funnel into the jar. Mold the clay around the top of the jar so that the funnel is held in place in the middle. Use enough clay to make a tight seal. Slowly pour water into the funnel. What happens to the water?

Use the pencil to punch a hole through the clay. Now what happens to the water?

The jar looked empty. However, something must have been inside the jar to keep the water out. It was air that took up all the space

inside the jar. Because there was no space inside the jar, the water stayed in the funnel. When you poked a hole through the clay, you allowed air to escape from the jar. This made room inside the jar for the water to enter. If air takes up space, then it must weigh something. How can you prove that air has **weight**?

Weighing Air

You will need:
- scissors
- string
- two balloons
- yardstick
- ribbon
- masking tape
- table
- pencil
- paper

Use string to attach a balloon to each end of the yardstick. Cut a 2-foot (41 cm) long piece of ribbon. Tie one end of the ribbon around the middle of the yardstick. Tape the other end of the ribbon to the side of the table so that the yardstick hangs freely underneath the table. Slide the ribbon so that the two balloons balance. When they balance, the yardstick will be level. With the pencil and

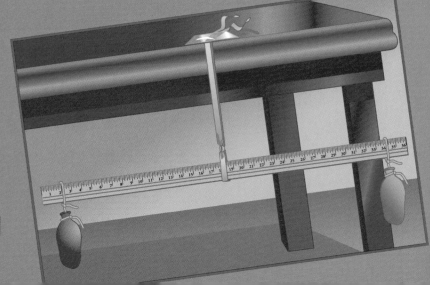

paper, make a note of where you placed the balloons.

Carefully remove one of the balloons from the yardstick. Blow up the balloon and tie it so that the air does not escape. Use the string to attach the balloon to the spot where it first was on the yardstick. What happens to the yardstick?

Before you blew up the balloon, the yardstick was level. But after you blew up the balloon, the yardstick tilted down toward the balloon filled with air. This means that the balloon filled with air weighed more than the empty balloon. So air has weight. Because it has weight, air should push against objects. What can air push against?

13

Keeping Water In

You will need:
- scissors
- thin piece of cardboard
- glass jar
- sink

Cut a square piece of cardboard large enough to cover the top of the jar. Completely fill the jar with water. Slide the cardboard across the top of the jar. Make sure that it touches the rim all the way around. Use one hand to hold the jar, and the other hand to hold the cardboard against the mouth of the jar.

You must use a jar that does not have any chips along its rim.

Quickly turn the jar upside down over a sink. Gently let go of the cardboard. What happens to the cardboard?

The cardboard stayed stuck to the jar, even though the weight of the water inside the jar pushed down on the cardboard. What, then, pushed on the cardboard so that it stayed in place? The air outside is pushing up on the cardboard. The force of the air pushing up was greater than the force of the water pushing down.

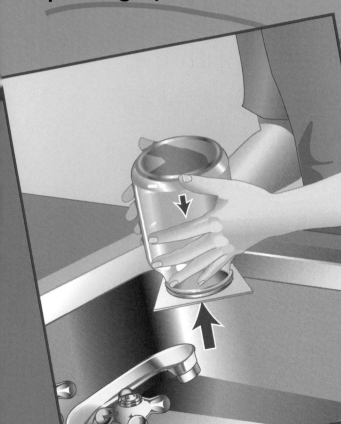

The larger arrow shows that air pressure pushing up on the cardboard is greater than the force of water pushing down.

Air is always pushing against things, including your body. On the ground, we don't feel the air outside pushing against our bodies because the air inside our body is pushing out with the same force. The force that air creates when it pushes against something is called **air pressure**. The air pressure inside your body is the same as the air pressure outside your body.

Air pressure is lower in the sky than it is on the ground. This is why the air pressure inside a plane has to be increased. Only then can the air pressure inside and outside the body be the same.

What Can Air Pressure Do?

You saw that air pressure can push with enough force to keep water inside a jar. Air pressure can do much more. For example, air pressure in the tires is all that holds your family's car off the ground. That's a lot of weight to hold up!

Air pressure is all that holds this SUV off the ground.

Is there a way to find out exactly how much weight is being held up by air pressure?

Holding Up a Car

You will need:
- an adult helper
- car
- tire pressure gauge
- chalk
- ruler
- calculator

Ask an adult to help you with this experiment. The car must be parked on a paved area. Use the tire gauge to measure the air pressure inside a tire. Use the chalk to draw an outline of one of the car's tires. Ask the adult to move the car away from the outline. Redraw the outline so that it has the shape of a rectangle.

Your outline will be a little curved because of the shape of the tire. Use the chalk to make the lines as straight as possible.

Measure the length and width of the rectangle in inches. Multiply these two numbers. This will give you the surface area of the tire touching the ground. The answer will be in square inches. For example, if the length of the rectangle is 7 inches, and its width is 4 inches, then 7 inches x 4 inches = 28 square inches. The surface area is then 28 square inches.

Multiply the length by the width to get the area inside the rectangle. Ask an adult for help with the math if the length and width are fractions.

Use a calculator to multiply the air pressure inside the tire by the sur-face area. For example, if the air pressure is 30 pounds per square inch, then 30 x 28 = 840. This tire is holding up 840 pounds. Because the car has four tires, air pressure is holding up 4 x 840, or 3,360 pounds.

Have you ever noticed that in the summer, the air pressure inside a tire seems higher than normal? Some of the air may have to be let out of the tire. In winter, the air pressure seems lower. Air must be added to the tire. Why does the air pressure in a tire change with the seasons?

Warming the Air

You will need:
- empty 2-liter plastic soda bottle with cap
- sink

Fill the bottle to the very top with hot water. Screw on the cap. Wait five minutes. Pour out the water and quickly screw the cap back on tightly. Watch what happens to the bottle. The water warmed the air inside the bottle.

Warm air also comes out of the bottle when you pour off the water.

When air gets warm, it expands, or spreads out. Because the bottle was sealed, the air had no place to go. However, some of the air escaped from the bottle when you opened it to pour out the warm water. When you put the cap back on, there was less air inside the bottle. This caused the air pressure inside the bottle to drop.

The larger arrow shows that the air pressure is higher outside the bottle.

The air pressure outside the bottle, however, did not change. When you poured out the warm water and replaced the cap, the air pressure outside the bottle was higher than the air pressure inside the bottle. The air outside pushed in harder than the air inside pushed out. The higher air pressure outside squeezed the bottle. What else besides temperature can change air pressure?

25

Making Air Move Faster

You will need:
- sheet of paper
- table
- ruler
- pencil
- transparent tape
- drinking straw

Place the paper on the table so that, as you look at it, the longer side is horizontal. At each end of the paper, draw two lines from top to bottom. The first line should be $1/2$ inch ($1\,1/4$ cm) from the edge of the paper. The second line should be 1 inch ($2\,1/2$ cm) from the edge of the paper.

Fold the paper along the lines so that each edge is in the shape of the letter L. Tape the paper to the table. Use the drinking straw to blow a steady stream of air underneath the paper.

What happens to the paper? Next, blow a stream of air across the top of the paper. Now what happens to the paper?

When you blew air underneath the paper, it curved downward. When air is moving, the air pressure goes down.

The larger arrow shows that the air pressure is higher above the paper, pushing it down.

The faster the air moves, the lower the air pressure. So blowing below the paper lowers the air pressure beneath the paper. The air pressure on top of the paper is higher, pushing it downward. When you blew air across the top of the paper, it curved upward.

The larger arrow shows that the air pressure is higher below the paper, pushing it up.

In this case, the air pressure was lower on top of the paper and higher underneath it.

The paper acts like the wing of an airplane. Making the air move faster across the top of the wing makes the plane go up. Making the air move faster across the bottom of the wing makes the plane go down.

Using Up the Oxygen

You will need:
- steel wool pad (without soap)
- small glass jar
- vinegar
- watch or clock
- large, shallow pan
- ruler
- food coloring
- spoon
- tall, narrow glass jar (such as an empty olive jar)
- pencil
- small drinking glass

Place the steel wool pad in the small jar. Cover the pad with vinegar. Let the pad soak for five minutes. While the pad is soaking, pour some water into the pan to a depth of one inch ($2\frac{1}{2}$ cm). Add several drops of food coloring and stir.

Drain the vinegar into the sink. Remove the steel wool pad. Pull apart the pad to separate the strands. Roll several strands into a ball.

Do not pack the strands tightly. The ball should be a little larger than the mouth

of the narrow jar. Use the pencil to push the ball to the bottom of the narrow jar. Turn the jar upside down and place it in the pan of water. Place the drinking glass over the narrow jar to keep it upright. Leave the jar in the water for 24 hours.

Make sure that nothing knocks over the narrow jar standing in the pan of water.

The next day, examine the jar. The colored water should have risen inside the jar. The steel wool should look rusted. Steel contains iron. Iron combines with oxygen to make **rust**.

As the oxygen inside the jar was used up to make rust, water moved in to take its place. After all the oxygen was used up, no more water could move into the jar. So the water took up the space that the oxygen once did. Notice how much air still remains in the jar. This space is taken up mostly by a gas called nitrogen. Is there anything else in air besides oxygen and nitrogen gases?

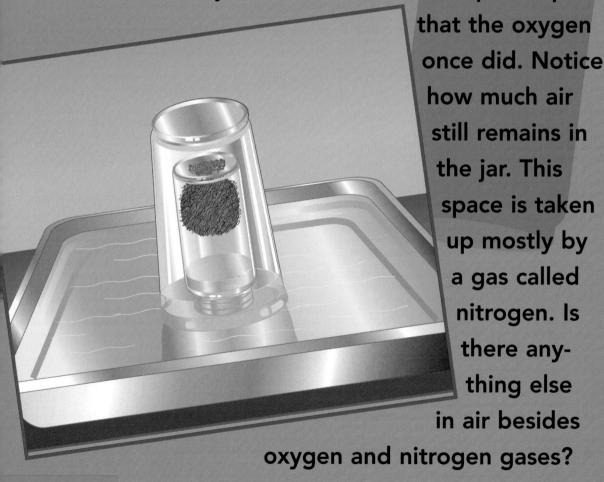

Experiment 8
Cooling the Air

You will need:
- two identical drinking glasses
- freezer

Place one glass in the freezer. Leave it there for at least one hour. Take it out of the freezer and place it next to the other glass that has been left at room temperature. Watch what happens to both glasses.

The glass left at room temperature should have remained clear and dry.

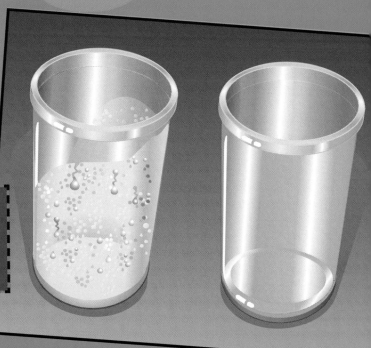

Can you see water droplets on the glass that was kept in the freezer?

However, the cold glass quickly became covered with drops of water. This water came from the air. Another gas in air is water **vapor**. When a vapor cools, it turns into a liquid. The cold glass caused the water vapor in air to turn into the water drops that you saw. What else is in air besides gases like oxygen, nitrogen, and water vapor?

When it boils, water turns into a gas called water vapor. This is commonly called steam.

Experiment 9

Catching the Dirt

You will need:
- 4 x 6 white index card
- ruler
- pencil
- plastic knife
- petroleum jelly
- small stones
- magnifying lens

Draw a 2-inch by 2-inch square on the index card. Use the knife to cover the index card with a thin layer of petroleum jelly. Find a spot outdoors where you can leave the card for 24 hours without it being disturbed. Place the card on the ground. Use the stones to keep it from flying away.

The next day, take the card inside. Use the magnifying lens to count the number of dirt particles that landed inside the square. Dirt is one of the things that can pollute the air. Experiment by testing different locations to see which one has the dirtiest air. Be sure to leave the cards out for the same length of time in every test.

Fun With Air

Because the air is filled with gases, it takes up space, has weight, and creates pressure. Air pressure can do some interesting things, like crushing soda bottles and allowing planes to take off and land. Now that you have learned some things about air, try this fun experiment.

Playing Tricks

You will need:
- a helper
- two balloons
- string
- scissors
- small bottle
- drinking straws

Blow up the two balloons. Use the string to tie the end of each balloon. Hold the balloons and ask a friend to use a drinking straw to blow air between the balloons. Your friend will probably be surprised to see that the two balloons move closer together rather than farther apart. Explain that blowing through the straw lowers the air pressure between the two balloons. Air pressure is higher on the opposite sides, pushing the balloons together.

Blowing through the straw lowers the air pressure between the ballons.

Next, fill the small bottle with water. Have your friend put two straws in his or her mouth. Tell your friend to put one of the straws into the water and to leave the other straw outside the bottle. Now ask your friend to suck the water out of the bottle through the straw. No matter how hard your friend tries, the water will remain in the bottle.

When you suck through a straw, you lower the air pressure inside your mouth. The air pressure outside is higher and pushes on the liquid in the bottle, forcing it into your mouth. However, air coming through the second straw outside the bottle prevents the air pressure in your mouth from getting lower. Because the air pressure inside your mouth is the same as the air pressure outside, you cannot suck up any water, no matter how hard you try.

To Find Out More

If you would like to learn more about air, check out these additional resources.

 **Books**

Ardley, Neil. **The Science Book of Air.** Harcourt Brace Jovanovich, 1991.

Gore, Gordon R. **Experimenting with Air.** Trifolium Books, 2000.

Murphy, Bryan. **Experiment with Air.** Two-Can Publishers, 2001.

Murray, Peter. **Air Science Tricks.** Child's World, 1998.

Oxlade, Chris. **Science Magic with Air.** Barron's Educational Series, 1994.

Silvani, Harold. **Experiments with Air.** Creative Teaching Associates, 1995.

White, Larry. **Air: Simple Experiments for Young Scientists.** Milbrook Press, 1996.

Environmental Protection Agency (EPA)
1200 Pennsylvania Avenue, NW
Washington, DC 20460
http://www.epa.gov/ region5/teachers/ curriculumair.htm

The EPA is the United States government agency in charge of protecting our environment, including the air. Log onto this site and check out the "Activities: Air" link.

The Exploratorium
3601 Lyon Street
San Francisco, CA 94123
415-EXPLORE
http://www.exploratorium. edu/snacks/snackintro.html

This site has a list of "snacks," which are short activities that you can perform at home. Some of these "snacks" deal with air.

Oklahoma Department of Career and Technology Education
http://www.okcareertech. org/aged/lab3_water_with_ air.htm

Learn how you can use air to lift water.

Science Museum of Minnesota
http://www.smm.org/sln/ tf/u/upupandaway/ upupandaway.html

Use a balloon to demonstrate that warm air rises.

Important Words

air pressure force of air pushing against something, like our bodies

gas substance made up of tiny particles that move quickly

rust substance that forms when oxygen reacts with iron

senses things such as touch, sight, smell, taste, and hearing, that we use to determine what is around us

weight measurement of how strongly an attractive force on Earth pulls on an object

vapor gas that can turn into a liquid when it is cooled

Index

Meet the Author

Salvatore Tocci is a science writer who lives in East Hampton, New York, with his wife, Patti. He was a high school biology and chemistry teacher for almost thirty years. As a teacher, he always encouraged his students to perform experiments to learn about science. Moving air helps to move his sail boat through the waters near his home.

Photographs © 2002: Corbis Images/Galen Rowell: 31; International Stock Photo/Ron Behrmann: cover; Photo Researchers, NY/Louis Goldman: 1; Rigoberto Quinteros: 4, 19, 22; The Image Bank/Getty Images: 9; The Image Works/Bob Daemmrich: 7; Visuals Unlimited: 2 (Mark E. Gibson), 17 (Jeff Greenberg), 29 (S. McCutcheon), 36 (Gregg Ozzo).

Illustrations by Patricia Rasch